Petrushkin!

Ron Charach

Ekstasis Editions

Canadian Cataloguing in Publication Data

Charach, Ron
    Petrushkin!

    Poems
    ISBN 1-896860-48-6

       I. Title.
    Ps8555.H39834P4   1999   C811'.54   C99-911101-9
    PR9199.3.C4727P4   1999

Cover photo: "Spin" taken by Ron Charach. *Cover design:* Mike Love
Author photo: Dan Roitner.

Acknowledgements:
A number of these poems first appeared in print in *The Lancet, The New Eng-land Journal of Medicine*, or *The Medical Post*. Other publications included *The Globe & Mail* and the literary journals *event, The Fiddlehead* and *Writer's News Manitoba*. "Picasso's 'Acrobat on a Ball'" appeared in The League of Canadian Poets anthology *Vintage 97*, published by Quarry Press. "A Ques-tion of Vitamins" appeared in the world anthology *Blood & Bone: Poems by Physicians*, published in 1998 by The University of Iowa Press, edited by Belli and Coulehan. "One LaughingUncle" appeared in the Internet magazine *The Alsop Review*.

       Thanks go to the editorial input and support of Susan Ioannou, Andy Patton, George Amabile and Alice Charach.

Published in 1999-2000 by:
Ekstasis Editions Canada Ltd.   Ekstasis Editions
Box 8474, Main Postal Outlet   Box 571
Victoria, B.C. V8W 3S1   Banff, Alberta ToL oCo

THE CANADA COUNCIL | LE CONSEIL DES ARTS
FOR THE ARTS | DU CANADA
SINCE 1957 | DEPUIS 1957

Petrushkin! has been published with the assistance of a grant from the Canada Coun-cil and the Cultural Services Branch of British Columbia.

This book is dedicated to Andy and Jan, Jon and Janice, Rhea and Alan, and Micheline and Allan.

Contents

Prologue:
What Is It about Curves?

What is it about curves
that makes drivers Indy up their speed
and two men walking towards each other
reach for secret holsters?
Why are rectangular dens
less homey than squares,
forcing the use of cherry-wood screens,
to slice ovals into arcs and circles
for a private, mathematical
taste?

What is it about Joseph Conrad,
who came to English late with a square's love
of philosophical abstractions, skin-shades and foreign accents?
Andy says Conrad "tries too hard"
'calumny, stratagem, inexpugnable,'
his armoury of words intentional
as platform shoes.
For what feels like a year
I sneak his precious *Lord Jim* on the subway.
Lately Patrick O'Brian steers my sea-faring,
his over-armed Sophie more than a match
for Conrad's creaky Patna
bulging with white-sheeted pilgrims,
or is she?

Whatever became of Nicholas Montsarrat's *Cruel Sea*
where bobbing blue-lipped sailors shouted
"*Russia! Prussia! Austria!*" as a giant sneeze
to keep alive in the freezing waters?

What is it about taste?
Why do some poets, corrupted by the tenor
of their own voices always read aloud their worst work,
saving the delicious obscurities
for the tiniest non-occasions,
an hour of solitude in an air-conditioned office
(square, but with a curved bay window).

There are days when the contents of my mind
are held together by duct tape.
At such times I take up reading
with its stiff-necked postures.
I tune in, say, to Szymborska's *View with a grain of sand*,
to 'Notes from a nonexistent Himalayan expedition.'

"So these are the Himalayas."

Acrobat on a Ball

A Mission to Sell Magazines

Manitoba, Gateway to the West.
Into the January glare, the morning deceptively sunny
for twenty-five below, my canvas bag bulged

"Wouldja like t'buy a mag'zine,
Liberty's a dime, Chatelaine's fifteen,
read how the Beatles are winning Canada's heart
and an interview with our own Beatle,
Pierre Elliott Trudeau!

Tripping over galoshes like a familiar
through drugstores, laundromats and beauty salons,
I was cute enough in those days
to be nicknamed Sandy for my hair.
More handsome but uneasy
was my older brother Aaron,
wearing his shaky confidence
like a second skin
—until we were *out there selling.*

No Canvassing or Soliciting.
Ignoring the signs we hit every business
until we arrived in Mecca,
The Hollywood Beauty Salon,
where, through a nimbus of hairspray and cigarette haze
no straight man, save Brad the Manager,
set foot.
Picking up wives and mistresses
husbands might tap their horns,
but waited prudently outside,
knowing faces were being reassembled
and embalmed.

On the main floor over a hundred women were mine
but under World War Two dryers,
in those insulated helmets
none but them could hear my spiel
or find the intentional trip-ups cute.
Worse, when the top of a row shook her head
she set off a slow chain-reaction.

But you!
Down in the pink fluorescent catacombs
you sold 20 *Liberties* and 10 *Chatelaines,*
never letting on that the ladies hanging their heads over sinks
were there to *dye* and had *hours*
to tear through magazines like silkworms
waiting for their roots to take.
And that Brad himself
bought "Ten of each—for The Shop".

Otherwise, beloved older brother,
who bought my first bike, first wristwatch,
who plied your trade so perfectly
you had no time for schoolwork,
who even the thrifty Scots at the *Free Press*
sent on First Prize trips to New York City,
Don'cha think ya could'a toad me?

Undimpled, I followed you out across tire-muddy trenches
into the crushy snow, combat rubbers leaking
'til my toes were frozen numb,
forty mags still weighing my left shoulder
to a slouch only tailors from South Italy would understand.

And though you would always remove a few,
all I could think of were the hours ahead
before our feet could thaw
and we could peel off the wool socks
and wait for the pink-red flow to return,
the painful tickle of a welcome home.

Press-ganged into paper routes
we were routed by a need for movie money, candy money.
We started early,
work,
that four-letter word,
someone else's song,
her smile warm the moment she saw me—but—
no reaching for her sacred purse.
To match Brad the Manager at Clarke Gabledom,
to outsell you, Aaron.
But the heavy glass doors up front
with the *Open/Closed* sign
returned us to the snowdrift glare
of a Winnipeg sun that always tries-*but-*
and a *God-but-it's-a-bitter* wind.

In Front of Kiev Steve

As Neptune in the school play
you must sail across their eyes,
never mind there's only Mom and Auntie looking up
with pride from the audience
or how makeshift the cardboard dolphin is.
Hang on to the trident for the backstage visit,
stay bright enough to outshine
disappointment.

Run and tell your father
just how much he missed, interrupt
his toasted sandwich lunch
in the bowels of the station, in front of
one of the three Steves.
Show off your daft Mediterranean accent
that delights the Black Sea immigrants;
for once, make Dad laugh,
with Kiev Steve joining in stitches.
"God-demmit, Sammy, he a card, dat little Hebrew boy from yours!"

because soon someone will be yelling
"What the—" or "Someone, help!"
because "TIM-BER!"
a triple-horned blood clot dislodges from one of Dad's legs
and sweeps straight through to his almighty core
stripping in seconds
any time left to know you,
all with one go-round
that makes him cough up his parsimonious life
like the toast and cheese
he lived on between binges,
between dreams of the solid little stucco he traded on Smithfield
for the decrepit wooden bungalow on Burrows.

Look back
at disappointment on a timer.
Hadn't you begun to soften
towards him, hadn't a more moderate part
begun to say, Go easy,
give your father time . . .
knowing, now, that death can douse any skillet,
you might have gladly let yourself become
soft-boiled eggs,
his loving son.

In the Valley of the Living

On my last run through the valley
I saw two young boys
holding the ends of two long curved branches
tossing back and forth a glistening garter snake,
practising a cruelty
older than psychology
on a slippery thing ten times longer
than Dad's.
I saw bees and wasps circling,
waves of bullrushes snapping,
whole stands of them levelling;

my race, perhaps,
to swell these stingy arteries to garden hoses,
vipers coiled 'round a leathery fist
that could tame me in ten seconds
with a pinch
or an intimate twist;
they too course through
a valley of the living,
unlit regions of inner man,
and, not knowing day from night,
they follow orders
from some pre-set timer device
that one day will click,
"Your last run"

Auto-Body Shop

In the auto-body shop
breathe in the glue and paint
like it was air, and hold your horses,
because the man who axed the question,
Coffee with milk? What are you, Mulatto? —
is Mario.
He can't smile.
He don't growl, is paid not to growl.
He wears a spotless work shirt
and when he's mad, his eyes narrow
and the mouth may close too full;
somehow you think about volcanoes.

Better to check out the calendars.
Out front, behind the counter
a lassie dog and a little Highland girl
from the people who make parts.
Out back, out the corner of your eye
a platinum blonde, naked under overalls,
with a rotweiler at her feet.

On the couch
just hangin' out
sprawls a lonely bull named Cornelio,
eight strands of hairs slicked across the dome,
huge soft muscles reminiscing.
He stops by every day, like Maurice,
a former boxer made of bones in a dark-hair suit,
coughing and coughing into the air
a thick visible cough that clears him space.

Aw, cummon! The Kid springs to his feet,
golden hair, tan corduroys,
bright yellow ski jacket, white-hot now
'cause they've put off his car (again) for later

but Mario melts him back to the vinyl.
His lower lip tightens:
You go to a Doctor,
and he tells you it'll be done
at such and such a time,
and you don' argue. Right?

I don't see no
fucken doctor, mumbles the kid
in a safety-valve way; he knows
the men with jobs and on disability come first.
To ease back in, and because
Mario's lower lip is stuck, his face
too many shades
too red,
he drops a question—about shocks and plugs,
as a feeler.

Swivel-chair flying back,
Mario rises,
steps well inside the kid's crease:
Y'know, Kid, he says,
I never noticed, but you're gettin'
mature.

One Laughing Uncle

Long after Uncle Simon died, Auntie Shailah boasted,
    "My Sarah's vorkin', my Hannah's vorkin',
        my Allan's vorkin'. . ."

One uncle, by trade an electrician,
in his late-thirties grew afraid of heights,
and holed himself in his room
with all the English classics
and dozens in Yiddish, Hebrew and Russian,
many of them humourous,
while his plump, pretty wife
trudged through snow in leaky rubber boots
door to door, business to business,
drumming up subscribers to
The Western Jewish News,
to feed their daughters and son.

Uncle, what makes an electrician fear
his heights, turns muscles into aching dough,
keeps him from driving a car,
owning a home, stripping paint
off a door?

Limping through my own late forties,
wife and children eating well
with no taste for herring, black bread
or prune juice in scalding water,
I look away from
his body's insurrection,
his explosive laughter,
borscht-belt surrender.

When She Swings

Returning to her glassy eyes mourning sudden deaths,
slipped discs, friends with freshly discovered lumps,
her wanderings to and from the unmade bed,
I hear her say, "I sleep the day away, no good,
no good."
Returning to her song before words
I wonder have I saved myself
swelling a continent to her concerns,
at fifty times her ample-bosomed thin-waisted size
I still feel her in my dreams.
Lines cut across and under
and straight through her eyes,
how she could twist my second-guesses
with her own surprising discoveries,
each one "a new lease on life".

Ow!
The glistening hook of her depressions
still catches me.

Picasso's "Acrobat on a Ball"

The young boy is poised on the ball, as if made of air.
His father looks on, a brooding stump of a man,
muscles heaped and knotted in rows along his back.
He ponders striking out at his smiling wisp of a son
who makes balance seem so effortless.

My eyes jerk back from the painting.
What am I doing?
Why an angry father, why a boy about to be struck?
Is it even a boy? Or is that a rose in the black hair?
Who is in peril, the slight child or my
enslavement to a distant past,
always reading in, reading in.
Must youth always be precariously poised,
at risk on a slippery ball?

Lapses

His face was a great divide.
One sensed a shifting of riverbeds and courses,
though no prevailing mood
could be lifted out.
I pulled at that face like an acrobat,
girded his huge belly, turning him into a redwood
with a begrudging smile.

One solitary synapse of smile fleets by
when I've had enough sleep or fish
to remember:
In the sun-warmed shallows of the lake,
how he suddenly swung to
letting me splash him,
to taking it like a sport; how modest,
these exceptions,
like lapses in a resolve.

Like a Goalie

for J.D.

Like a rookie goalie
who dressed in set order in the locker-room
to bend and lace his skates,
groaning under heavy padding
drenched in perspiration,
I rock my head to keep the neck muscles loose.
Like Patrick Roy, I talk to my lucky goalposts
(a goalie's best friends)
and nervously clear the front of the crease
of mounds of ricochet.
Dousing the neck to cool off between lunges,
I choose a single player on the other team
to keep off the scoreboard;
a game-within-a game lessens
the sting of one blowing by me.

No brooding on predecessors,
goalies who got branded wing-nuts or flakes,
because before the advent of masks
they were crazy enough to hang
in front of Bobby Hull slapping rock-hard pucks at 140 m.p.h.,
in those early days of curved sticks
when not even Hull knew where
his shots would end.
Yet they laughed at Jacques Plante
behind his makeshift effort to save face.
No wonder Glen Hall got the jitters before games
and carried a retching towel.
Those foolish fans, who think the goalie
is the least conditioned player on the team!

If ever I get to play you again
I won't cower in my crease.
I'll have a mouth-guard, shin-pads,
neck-guard, kidney pads,
jock-strap and cup,
perhaps a Prozac mask, for improved control,
a sixth sense for whenever
you're hanging near my net;
or standing in the bleachers booing,
holding your nose and widely waving your arm
to clear the air of my bad play.
This time I'll keep you off the scoreboard,
deflect any shit you slap my way.

Our Lady of the Bumblebees

You are sunbathing on a worn red blanket
in the tiny yard backing the Burrows house.
It's Sunday morning,
and Dad, as usual,
is off at his older sister's
eating leftovers from her Sabbath dinners.

Your lovely tanned face—my face—
is turned towards the sun,
long lashes closed, nostrils slightly flaring
as you revel in a prairie summer day.
Around you flurry bumblebees,
alighting on the dandelions and clover,
buzzing near your slender feet,
flying low over bare arms glistening at your sides.

Rows of sticked tomato plants and luxuriant rhubarb
take up a third of the yard to the edge of your blanket.
Some mornings I watch you putter in the planted shade,
turning the soil, pretty as a sweater-girl with a watering can,
ignoring around you bees and long-legged wasps
—while little Aaron and I run like the dickens
whenever one comes at us, screaming "*Beenen! Beenen!*"
our own made-up Yiddish word.

Now and then, across the wide-spaced fencing
the Ukrainian *babushka* next door gives gardening advice,
pointing, "Dis is veeds; dat is no veeds."
In exchange, you use Ukrainian words you've worked
to say perfectly, the usual weather banter:

"*Tepleh! Zimneh!*" "It's hot out! It's cold!"
"*Moszhe dozshe; mozshe schnee.*"
"Maybe rain; maybe snow,"

jewels in your cosmopolitan crown
that always make the neighbours smile.
Though after we were given carrots from their garden,
you made me surpass you, marching me off
with a memorized mouthful,
"*Moya mama khazala zshankuyu za morkvah.*"
"My mother would like to thank you for the carrots,"
making up for decades of Old Country anti-Semitism
that was, in the end, who knows whose original sin.

Backyard beauty of many tongues, are you the one
I'd one day call Lady of the Dumb *I Love You's*,
because you seldom came to my defense,
though you loved me—you—
who never made it into the history books,
but modelled for us,
a solitary poise that was its own reward,
Our Lady of the Bumblebees.

Oucho the Gaucho

Vote Prairie

for George Amabile, author of "Prairie"

What names for the sacred grain
whose windswept tops form waves of light and shadow
to grace a grown child's meditations:
wheatfield soul, frenchkiss alfalfa
john barleycorn, mangiacake rapeseed,
italo canola?

May they remain anonymous
as a populist ground-swell,
knots of farmers dozing at town-hall meetings
while their wives applaud the C.C.F. socialist dream
of universal progress, elusive
as billowy cloudforms shifting . . .

a prairie vote for vast potential
space no minister or congregation can fill.
Not a promenade's gold towers
reflected in a river,
a tanker edging past
harbour junks and sampans,
nor tiers of luminiscent accordions
played by tuxedoed gentlemen from Rio,
where they also have a prairie.

"Oucho the Gaucho",
I named him
long before I encountered Brooklyn's *Promenade,*
Hong Kong's dreamy harbour
or the gaudy exuberance of *Forever Tango.*

Oucho votes
not for some chatty Queen Street space-girl
with a cell phone cradled between
"the largest free-standing breasts in the world,"
nor a CN tower-by-the-dome
leering with gargoyle fans,

but for a prairie child
squinting from a bicycle into the smoky heat
at the grand indeterminate space,
the far-off convergence
of parallel trains.

Flying Stanley Home

My painter friend, a lanky high-principled man,
is not unlike his great-uncle
at peace in the hold of the plane.
He paints the inside of abandoned silos a "sweet blue,"
and is as devoted to the intricacies of canvas
as his Great-uncle Stanley was
to parliamentary procedure's fragile weave.

The only non-government member
ever to sit on the Privy Council,
even after a stroke snared half of him and dimmed his speech,
he was asked by the Commons to stay on, and observe
as a collective conscience,
representative-in-perpetuity of Winnipeg North Center.
He fought alongside David Orlikow
for the worker, for pensions, unemployment insurance,
single mothers and their kids.
"Thank you for giving me a reason to go on living,"
said a tall, stooped, but unbowed Stanley Knowles.

It's a muggy day for a state funeral,
hard on the back and feet, all the standing around,
as the great man's two grown children and their families in black
labour to shake five thousand hands.
Construction workers doff hard-hats,
matrons in silk and pearls look stricken
for the man who more than anyone
dwelled in the House,
treating everyone from the Prime Minister
to the café cashier with respect;
who, when hungry, would sometimes treat himself
to a sandwich of plain roast beef on white.

From Ottawa the family, including my painter friend,
fly Stanley Knowles to his other home, Winnipeg,
on Chrétien-and-The Queen's own plane,
deadpanning it 'Air Force One'
ironically royal treatment:

"Stanley would approve of going
cargo class . . "

Roughing It

Where's a good outhouse when you need one?
You have to raid Uncle Dick's memory,
for the pilot, who, when his compass broke,
flew low over the outhouses, knowing
that these houses of worship nine times out of ten face East,
"to catch the morning sun—when you need it."
He tells of three-and four-holers
"each hole a tad bigger than the next,
to accommodate both granny and gramps,
not to mention the newest little graduates
from the chamber-pot."
He tells of crescent-moon windows and stars
cut into doors designed to open in,
"so you could halt a sudden intruder
with an outstretched leg.
For a view, you had a choice of spiders."

"Were there regular windows too, Uncle Dick?"

"You wouldn't want 'em. Too drafty."
The thermal factor nets more memories,
of several in a large family needing to sit at once.
"With all those over-clothes you had your privacy.
After, you could track the drainage paths
by the lushness of the back-yard vegetation.
You hoped the guy who decided where to build
considered the well."

From the kitchen I can hear him retell the best of Chic Sales,
a vaudevillian who made hay out of outhouse jokes
in a best-seller called *The Specialist.*
Specialist of a different kind, I hoist shirtsleeves
for another after-dinner load of dishes.
It's a matter of pride to return them to a pristine state.
I think of the eco-friendly no-flush modern toilets
this morning at McArthur State Park,
how, to approach them, we had to walk beneath silent
hovering eight-inch golden orb-weaver spiders.
And recall how the prairie passenger trains of my youth
dropped their effluent straight on the tracks,
no flushes allowed 'til the train left the station.
Riding the rails,
one more way of roughing it.

Five-pin

At the bowling alley
we slip on the regular maroon and taupe issue,
shoes too ugly to steal,
and head for lane 24, far from the smokers.
It's hard to adjust to holding back
while the machine does the clearing
and avoid a premature bowl,
worse in the days when kids with attitude
reset the pins.

Bowling. The last sport
I can keep up with my athletic son.
His back is thickening with muscle,
neck and shoulders, though protruding like Dad's,
see better around corners, down shiny hardwood lanes.
My daughter, at seven,
still plonks the ball along the floor,
and not discouraged, bowls on.
My wife and I team up against the kids,
our hearts less thrilled than theirs
when the electronic scoreboard
greets a strike with a jumping Jack.

I want to replay the Coen Brother's *The Big Lebowski*,
about three loveable losers in an L.A. seedy-rich as Sodom
who share ten-pin as their karma.

Our family rarely goes to movies,
but we do *Clue* and *Scrabble*—better—*Upwards,*
where stacking letters can metamorphose one word into another,
the way I'd like to transform this Bowlerama
and Smiley, its mustachioed manager
with the earring and smoker's cough
and Coke machine that demands exact change
and around each pair of lanes,
the long semicircular plastic benches
that make my bottom ache.

What I'd never change are those crazy balls,
marbled orange and black fantasy swirl
or a dowdier, meaner lunar-looking gray-on-white,
these older ones blending to a mucky hue
more likely to strike paydirt.
The Hallowe'en ones tend to knock out the middle pin
like a pegged front tooth,
leaving four standing tall in derisive attention,
Go ahead, try to get us with one shot, make our day.
Perhaps they're just paying homage to physics,
snubbing a less-than-perfect vector.

It's the kind of thing the Coen Brothers did so well in *Fargo*:
a loser of a con-artist tries to mulch a corpse
in a backyard wood-chipper,
as a tired, very pregnant female cop
takes on whatever comes her way.
Her North Dakota accent is flat as a prairie bowling lane
after it and every last one of life's unsmooth surfaces
has been thoroughly buffed
and rebuffed.

Lime-green

Flaring into vogue
poor lime-green
finds no easy matches,
and is left closeted
to savour the tang
of the peculiar.

From a height of platform sandals,
pure lime-green screams *Piss off*! to navy,
ugly and direct
as Howard Stern.
(Help me side-step poetry's
relentless
cross-referencing.)

Let me wear lime
at the height of day,
do battle with lemon-yellow, russet and tangerine.
Lift me high above
the sand-grain multitude
of dowdy birds.
Save me
from love affairs
with the pale-green neutral cast of money.
Give me the hue and cry
of words!

Baldy's Song

Sing
shell of cognition, cogitation.
Sing "no grass grows . . "
Sing chamber pot of tyrants,
skull of Yorick,
skele-dome.
Sing
God's own repository
shining through bone.

Bouffante Agonistes

As if by a giant dryer I'm blown
by how many women out there
dye their hair, and pose
with countenance severe
beneath a youngster's coiffured crown.

'til I spot their balding paunchy men
in lukewarm water, clowns
who crane at girls no older
than their daughters.

A Friend from the Deep South

With graying blonde hair
and neatly trimmed goatee,
you're charming as Shelby Foote in *The Civil War* series,
and though overactive with tics and twitches,
a regular Cotton-eye Joe on the dance floor
sweeping other men's wives off their feet.
Yet you tell me how, one night,
on a deserted beach in the Pacific
you and a lover were *wakened*
by the light of the Milky Way.

Next morning after a long swim
lazing on a slab of granite
overlooking the lodge,
you nod at a huge flat rock
that lilts with each incoming wave.
"I've never before seen a big rock
placed so it moves like that."
Same morning, you point out
a tall blonde lining up for burgers at The Sizzler.
She's wearing a see-through cotton dress.
"Do you think she knows it is?" I ask,
and without thinking, you answer,
"You bet."

Excuse Me

From a height of roller blades,
"Excuse me," she says,
shaking away a blonde ringlet and tearing through
my not-a-morning-person fog,
"can you tell me what street this is?"
"Harbord," I answer.
She nods, and shapely
muscled calfs and thighs push off.
I want to shout after her,
"Your smile is the only thing
that could wake me!"
But my comic head says,
 "Well, *ex-kyooze meeee!* . . ."
Not much comic out this early,
when a caseload of complexes
awaits me like a squatting bull
that has hung up its blades forever.

Exchange

My eyes are pulled, not to a nude on a beach,
but into the frothy waves caressing
the *zaftig* blonde in **Les Femmes Erotiques**,

She rises, naked woman from the sea,
and with a haughty crease of thighs
bends over the foaming surge

answering my aching gaze
with a wink of flesh
and a slash that slays.

French Romance

On a moonless neutral night
it was eerie easing up to her
two huge mascara'd eyes.
She squeezed me tight as a colonial,
apologizing about "ze menstruel blood"
and warned about
a heavy flow
(she must have had an I.U.D.)

She let me have it every way I dreamed
twisting Left, and even further Right,
murmuring *de riens*, like *Vichy*, and *Boche* and *Maoiste*,
a horn of plenty from behind;
and all because I didn't mind.

I'd been shafted by Uncle Sam a million times;
it felt good to play the man again.
Until I felt the gooey oozing down my thigh
like scarcely refined Arabian crude!

I told her *Get out*,
just plain get out!!
I'd know *that* smell anywhere,
the smell of petrol politics.

I sat on the cold white bowl for hours
rubbing in varsol, tearing the hair from my legs.
'Round my ankles the tarry mass crept upward
like something from *The Blob*!

'til my hapless matted one-eyed friend
winked free, to lewd refrain,
"In the Land of France . . ."

Silent Couple

"Questa
coppia e in silenzio.
Questi abiti
parlano."

In the Not-For-Admission waiting-room:
a striking young couple,
he seated with his back to her,
she standing dancer-like behind him,
her hand on the back of his chair
as she stoically stares.

His hair slicked back with gel,
he sports a starched black shirt and matching trousers.
She is a heron of a blonde,
her furry sweater's neckline plunges
over a halter-top, and well below.

A see-through floral skirt
traces her sinewy thighs
down a blurred fault-line
to shoes tied-on, stiletto-heeled
anti-personnel devices.

Happily, a translation is supplied:
"This couple is silent.
These outfits talk."

after an ad for ANTONIO FUSCO
in *Vanity Fair*

Pioneers of Puberty

To Laurence Inch,
who after a long summer vacation
debuted in nude swim with a thickened root
fringed by a shock of red filaments
from which tautly hung a pair of golf balls,
yet, for all that, wound up
one of the shorter males in our class,

To gawky Kathy,
who wore party-hats beneath her long neck
the boys found irresistably funny,
and Belva, so maternally endowed
we couldn't pry our eyes away
from her areolar stare,

To my own neotenous group of three,
prepubertal to the bone, advocates of the silly,
who tried, with flashlights
under bathroom-lock
to speed the stubborn mystery,
boasting prematurely,
"Haven't *you* creamed yet?"

as though it were a subtle variation
on pissing, and not a shock
to the system to send us reeling
for a recovered older brother, who would smile
and say, "yup—that sure sounds like it."

A moment of silence
for those who made their fellow children mothers,
for those obliged to open still-slender thighs
to surgical equipment and scorn,
for the misconceived
whether born and mis-mothered
born and surrendered,
or forever and ever
unborn.

Petrushkin!

Millions of Yahrzeit Candles

All around the world
millions of *yahrzeit* candles burn
for my father, who never heeded
the high-flying wispy breaths
of a red mackerel sky.
Smoke wafts from the mouths
of passers-by whose lips are dry and cracked,
as if they would flicker my father's name
if it suddenly came to them.
Some have small-vessel disease yet will smoke on
even through amputations.

Like them, Pa rolled "pills,"
stringy tobacco in ultra-thin *Vogue* papers,
slim pillars in a barely balanced life,
and nursed a late-night glass of Coke as he prepared
for another night-shift in the windowless basement
of the high-domed railway station,
breathing in and out his own smoke
like the burning bush raging
against its confinement
that he was.

Timing

Out front of the Gothic hospital
the gray-bearded professor in a three-piece tweed,
returned from delivering a speech
destined to save a million lives,
bends to tie his laces.
Around the corner rushes
a tall lean man
with a baby in a snugli on his back.
"Not on my time!" he hollers,
and with a swift kick, sprawls the professor
onto the manicured lawn.
As he climbs past the bright shirts and skirts
crowding in to check the commotion,
his baby wails
as her father scales the turret
to his place on the hospital spire.

Three Dreams

I'm studying anatomy,
a young post-partum mother lying supine on a table,
is she dead?
We examine her closely,
her iodinated belly under a veiling fan
that moves her downy hairs in the tiled room.
Suddenly in walks Dr. Morton
sporting a cigaret ash three inches long.
Hello, Dr. Morton, I say,
but all he does is tap and butt out
on my spotless white consultant's coat,
then disappear.
A joke?

The second also takes place in a hospital room.
I am tonguing a honey-blonde
who awaits an operation.
We are heating up, but in the next bed
lies another patient, around fifty, a man in a plastic bra.
He interrupts us, then sneers,
"Don't let me disturb
your masturbation."
Is he/she also snickering?

The third is set on a drizzly day.
There are two heads lying on the ground,
a muddy street from the Wild West.
The clever bearded heads are either disembodied
or buried neck-deep in the mud.
Some drunks approach these hapless heads
and splash water on their faces
'til they sputter.

I refuse to dream about the foreign resident
who, frustrated by a missed diagnosis,
dissected his dead patient right there in the bed,
on the spot, and was promptly relieved
of his license.

It is almost as punishing, waking up.
Ice-cold water swallowed straight from the fridge
rises painful through my head.
I savour the silent aftermath,
and like the clear bulb beaming thinly at the back,
try to shed a little on thought behind closed doors, like light.

Hal

How many are there like you,
awkward six-four mantis frame,
bobbing head high above the crowds, or folded
high-kneed on a seat in an endless subway,
a last worn volume of Dostoevsky to your name?
You changed appearance with each mood,
a series of brilliant heads:
some hairy, some shaved,
each anguished, and off the mark.

Your inventions!
A straw hooked up to a vacuum cleaner
pulled snot faster than a head-cold replaced it.
And your performance art:
a slide-show of wrinkled blank pages, magnifications
of things no one would think to show,
set to music.

Your suicide, however long predicted, was sudden,
like the white-water rafting
you tried once on a lark,
complete strangers howling across you
as you offered your finely shaped skull
and proud tartar cheekbones
to the cool passages
marked by rocks.

Hurdler

View of a minor poet disappearing

I met you just once, long enough to guess
you had plunged into back-to-back drinks,
strong cigarets, and day-night reversals,
so that no one could help.

Above a compact body, a tight face
constricted with the agony of too many small trials.
An ironic name, you had,
Singleman, was it?

Oddly immune to put-downs of your work,
you praised the books of other writers.
In a way you were self-possessed, poised
to spring from the starting blocks
of "one last try,"

to go with the original bad start
into a blind leap forward
cutting circles in the air,
keeping head well down,

as good hurdlers must,
your hung-over eyes fixed on death,
the one remaining hurdle.

The Diet of Stefan

A Vegan and a rawist, Stefan lives exclusively
on green peppers, tomatoes and nectarines,
has nothing but contempt for
"dead vitamins and minerals
the body cannot use."
Warned by his physician ex-wife in '85
that he would be dead within a year,
he approaches the millenium in triumph
laced with fear.

Once he confided that he had "psychic bangs".
"Pangs?" On being corrected,
I thought he meant those small but complex universes
spawned by the unconscious mind.
No, the errant tendrils of brain
that festooned his eyes
whenever his plastic skullcap
was pulled away with force.

He made me think of Luther
at the Diet of Worms,
judged by the Western world
yet recanting nothing,
warning his interrogators
how dangerous it would be if to ignore his conscience.
Spirited into safe hiding
by Frederick the Wise,
he rewrote the New Testament version
still used by the Church that bears his name.
Later, as if struck by internal lightning,
he railed against the Jews
for their failure to ingest
the newer, more wholesome
homilies.

Petrushkin!

We are spinning on a globe, Petrushkin,
where the ultimate Disney set
is Alcatraz Island,
where thirty-nine Heaven's Gate cultists
shed their Earthly containers to hitch a ride
on a spaceship behind the Hale-Bopp comet
to a new home near Sirius.

A cloudy blue globe whose spin no one feels
but melancholics on a switch day
or burned-out manics recalling
the old high-flying ways.

Even you, roynish Petrushkin,
thimble-sized in a pseudo-Russian hat,
white scarf unfurled like angel wings
twirling on the end of my flaky thumb,
swirl an unfamiliar potato smell
with orange and yellow halos around black balls
that lure nerve-doctors to my temporal lobes.
See how they parade in starched white coats
and keep me up all night
and crown my scalp with needles
in the hope of catching a trace of you
bald-faced, wide-eyed,
mid-parody—

The Mind

The addled mind bites down
on the sacred/scared flowers of the imagination.
Not that the mind is an assassin,
a ball of wizened gray suspended in fat,
trailing long-haired nerves
down an arching tailbone,

re-programmed from birth by religion,
hostile father or analyst
who, hour after fifty-minute hour,
corroborates what your aunt Polly
could have told you,
nor an organ pining for frappaccino
while loathing the fellow subway rider down the bench
for his rich early-morning cough.

This is, after all, the deliberate mind
that selects scream-yellow tinteds
to modify wintry grays,
that shelters from the blinding light of April
behind neutral green shades,
the mainframe mind that chatters incessantly
like Netscape cleaning up a 'disk cache'
or some other extended neuro-anatomy
the soul never knew it had,

the testy mind
that demands bifocals at forty,
that bids inquisitors to 'run that by me again',
that confuses directions, reads Alzheimer's
in a forgotten name,
the acrobatic mind
betrayed by distant shin splints,
the recumbent mind that fades
when it should be 'concentrating on the breath'.

Less distant from the heart, troubled
by thirty spikes of pressure per night,
the mind of a poet races
at cross-purposes with workaday minds,
and is loathe to justify lapses,
to apologize for its allegiance
to a lunar calendar.

Such a mind would stay awake dreaming prayers
for the ovaries and breasts and prostates of close friends,
were it not all so liturgical.

Freud's Face

Here again is Freud, on a subway poster
to advertise the film series Rendezvous with Madness,
red-and-green 3-D glasses superimposed
on his sepia image holding a fat cigar.

Everyone takes a turn adorning his face
emblematic as the sphinx.
Ralph the cartoonist pulls it to rubber
from an orgiastic nightmare,

Phyllis the biographer
stuffs his cheeks with cotton,
and parades him
as a conspiring Mafia don

while a feminist journal
remolds him as a Grumpy the dwarf
tumescing like a Plathian Daddy
in an itchy-looking three-piece-tweed.

He too gazed in the mirror,
grieved first the gray in his beard,
then the painful surgeries
to his critic-slaying jawbone.

Opponents haul him from his century,
judge him
by their decade's norms
as they say he judged others

even while being repeatedly branded
the ultimate
godless
Dirty Jew.

The Appendix

"Scapegoat of the bowel",
you tickled and burned inside the body
causing as much mischief as the wandering womb.
How many with pellets and big wind in their bowels,
too cowed by life to pump nervous energy into gain,
went under the knife for a 'chronic appendix'?
How many pathologists fudged reports on normal specimens
to block patient suits and irate surgeons?
"Two kids of appendix," went the old joke,
"acute" and "for revenue only."

The psychotherapist also ferrets a worm,
the dark serpent of negative thinking
waving one of its archaic heads,
be it precious phobia, tormenting obsession
or absurd delusion,
perhaps just a long piece of unfinished business
dangling from the oblong psyche
like the tail that moves a mechanical dog
until busted, it and loses its spring.

"The ego is first and foremost a body ego"
True, Dr. Freud, but comparing the bowel to the brain,
even in the reign of the chronic appendix,
sounds hopelessly anal.

after Edward Shorter's *From the Mind into the Body*

Shiatsu

Tetsuro-*san* knows when to, and not to
make conversation, when to let
the piped-in Japanese flutes hold sway.

I am here to re-route my *chi*,
to pool toxins into bruises cleared with capillary ease
as he redraws the map of soma,
new capital cities, all my world's pain
sweetly, deliciously squeezed
to fine points of surrender

as the dark night yields
to the press of day.

John Goodman Special

Morning Motif

Above ground the sun shines
but below the city, wheels screech
as the train scrapes a tight turn
swaying strap-hangers like me,
stirring a thrum of nerves
that shoot sparks down the thighs.

The slight Japanese man with the faultless posture,
he could be *sensei* Kashiwazaki
who broke both elbows doing a judo throw
and was forced to develop new techniques
for on-the-ground fighting.

A South-Asian grandpa, also straight-backed,
his winter tuque uneasily topping
a thick Indian accent, points to the subway map:
"How far in minutes to march to the next stop?
And the next? I could march.
To me it is nothing; I am a military man!"

Vale tudo.
"Anything goes." Portugese? Latin? "Ill-health"?
Or a free-style form of grappling, as in "extreme fighting,"
but with discipline,
as in extreme public transit.

Last night was pill-free,
a night of dream fragments and fitful awakenings.

Where are you in this parade
of specimens too poor
or too fearful or too aggressive
to drive?

Buskers

All the world's a station,
And all the men and women merely buskees.

Artistic eyes assess him as he plods along the walkway
clodhopper galoshes slowing his pace,
eyes that can spot a sucker for Peruvian flutes
or a mandolin played with gusto.
Between breaths they look up from performance
as he draws near, fingering coins in his pocket
lest he accidentally part with a loonie.
They ignore the spasm of a hasty toss,
the diffident nod of a tweed cap.

At the office, the glamorous Director
reminds him that she comes from Lithuania.
He doesn't say, "I'd love to go,"
but prefers his Lithuanians
reshaped by the soil, water, air
and fire of his own mystery places,
prefers listening for the remains of a brogue
in a B.C. union leader's voice,
the nasal twang of a displaced Southerner in a parka,
the slapping wave of a Russian Jew's contempt
for his fellow Russian Jews
who have been here "fif-tyeen yeers",
yet still won't flatten their vowels.

On his way home from work
he keeps back his shoulders and his chin tucked in
marching past another crew of performers,
each juggling their native land's bests and worsts,
each nursing a dream
of a long voyage home
and nothing but first class all the way—

En Route

Driving to the poetry reading on a bright spring evening,
and YAAAA—-HOOOOO!
a 16-ish skateboarder,
dark-eyed in hooded sweatshirt and headphones,
high on ecstacy, crystal meth, mania or April
flies down the steep slope of Bathurst Street,
free-falling through the red light, challenging vans
and other urban assault vehicles
to weave.

A devotee of Devo, raves, bands
like Butt-Hole Surfers, Age of Electric-Limblifter?
Or home-made D.J. Jungle music,
a boarder's Indie label, with mid-day screamers
striking three or four simple chords to the background
of a relentless drum,
music written for distortion pedal.

So convincing a flirt with death
he survives and I drive on.
If I owned a cellular I could call 9-1-1
en route to the poetry reading
where again life will thumb its nose at death
at a remove.

Poetry Reading

(W)rites of Spring.
Begin the ascent, a deep dark stairway
opens onto a seedy field of pub,
nothing modern but a popcorn machine
and two huge black speakers.
A full-size pool table under a Tiffany lamp
holds stacks of slim poetry books
that remain undisturbed all evening.
A cooler-than-thou emcee
shy poet himself, thin and handsome with Christ-like pallor
and Albrecht Duhrer hair,
bottle of beer in one hand, pack of smokes in the other,
delivers the perfunctory intros.
The audience is straight out of Charles Bukowski,
a pack of students coerced by a workshop leader,
a few couples, friends of a friend of,
a cluster of older women poets
(old poets never retire, they ride out
an extended metaphor) suffering
from such image-fatigue their expressions say,
"Go ahead, see if you can move us,
and for how long.

Not that any poet would want to spray
It is now after the end of the world
on a concrete abutment on Spadina,
or snap in half two freshly planted trees
on the cobblestone boulevard
— same guy?

But we're in for a musical interlude,
a guest appearance by a well-known local singer
straight off a downtown musical run,
his velvety *a capella* tenor
a gift to fill mere wordsmith's hearts
with envy.
Notwithstanding Leonard Cohen, what can a poet sing?
(My own attempt on the missa luba from the movie *If*
wouldn't cut it.)

It's different at a poetry reading,
say, from a packed subway car
where loud snorting noises would make you look around
for a parent horsing with his kid
rather than some tubercular homunculus.

As the singer takes his seat
(we know he won't be staying to the end)
who will be first to read?
Several have asked to benefit from all the fresh ears,
so long as they're not the very first.
Who wants to be a warm-up act?
Best read early, and escape
the so-so images, the high ratio of words
to real poetry, the line-up of young Turks
who fancy themselves incarnations of the Beats,
like "the lovely young 'performance' poet,"
(what does that make the rest of us?)
who travels with her own male percussionists.
She reads early so her accompaniment won't have to stick around,
and, though all were warned "Keep it to five minutes"she luxuriates
like a peony for half an hour,
about "children in far-off lands
we don't even know the names of."

Several times she chants,
"There are ravens in my hair,
There are ravens in my hair!"
Did she say raisins?
Ah, but she's slender,
her voice is clear and strong,
and one of her boyish men plays a long painted gourd.

Next up, the earnest middle-aged professor by day,
or a doctor (never a tax lawyer or accountant)
who reads with such sonorous sincerity
the mind wanders off to his secret life
in the other profession.

Best for last, the besotted elder statesman of the form,
fiddling with the mike to his own specs,
and, though no Al Purdy, a true Beat,
who can override our resentment at the hour.
Stocky, he wrote a book on Hemingway,
his balding head is fringed with fly-away hair,
he sports a seaman's beard, closely cropped.
We try hard not to think 'He's not going to live much longer'
as he flips through the pages of his latest,
his lengthy monologues less amusing than the poems
in which a car packed with screaming teens pulls off the highway
across fields full of sweet green peas,
"something you can't do any more in America," he points out.
Here, here!
His fare is lush and topical, and high calorie. He celebrates
sex. He hangs out
at pubs and parties and cafés.

But tomorrow's a work day.
Having planned to leave during the third break,
I won't get to hear the striking black-bearded poet from Sarajevo
two tables over, sitting with his pretty translator-wife.
Go-ran—is that his name?
For, though I don't have asthma
and the kids are no longer babies,
I need a good hour to decompress before sleep,
poetry can light my brain to the hum
of an all-nighter, always dangerous in April.
Once home, it takes time
to toss my clothes in the washer,
hang my vest in the furnace room
to be rid of cigaret reek, and then shower.
Half the smoke seemed to come from the chain-
smoking poet from Sarajevo,
But who can blame him?
And where there's smoke . . .
there's poetry.

Airport Express

On the airport express to Victoria
five days of rain suddenly breaks into intense sun.
The driver's a friendly 350-pounder
who flicks suitcases like picnic baskets,
a gentle giant you have to trust,
but for worries about shortened life-spans
as he speeds the bus around stands of Douglas fir
— flashes of a John Goodman role.
If this guy ever charged you'd think '*Grizzly!*'
and helplessly tinkle your little silver bell.

It's a thrill to drive through poet country
seated next to a pretty cadet
who's tied her service hat around her bun,
all slim waist, taut butt and no revolver.
Around the world thousands like her
trying to keep spots off their uniforms.
Not like our driver. Overheated and casual,
he wipes rivulets from his brow
with a tree-trunk forearm
on this rare West Coast scorcher of a day.

We weave around the tight cluster of downtown hotels.
At each stop he rearranges the luggage
on the three-tiered rack,
at a thirteen buck fare, there are plenty of stops
He rears up like that metal bear in the arcade rifle game,
to take on an old lady's patterned valise,
"You got your life in here, ma'am?"
Two stops later he's hauling down a huge green metal box,
grinning, "Your brother in here?"
Finally he calls out, "Empress Hotel!
We made it — Empress!"
My final stop comes later, the poets' meeting "Crystal Court Motel"

a nondescript two-story out of the Fifties,
its approach so narrow he lets me off by the curb.
Should I tip him? Few people do.
Are we keeping the covenant of the bargain fare,
or breathing a sigh of relief?

None of us is an airport limo type
any more than he's *ursus horribilis*,
or a John Goodman special.

Seattle Shine

Stopping for a shine in a small patch
of neighborhood off Pike Street Market,
three lean young Afro-Americans standing around
the well-muscled shine man, all shaved bald heads,
hands in the pockets of loose-riding jeans.
Mr. Shine-man motions me, pale skinny guy,
onto his stand, barely balancing,
the tension shooted up my grounded Canadian leg.
Will they roll me the second I pay?
(Pre-counted money slid into
a wallet-less pocket before I stepped up
for my shine?)

"Hey, man, you-all seen Griffley Jr. hit three past the wall?"
Raps with his buddies as he does my shoes
— with a toothbrush! — dabbing at an opened can,
doing the loaves-and-fishes on just those tiny patches
that *cry* for a shine,
making do,
and buffs my scuffed Rockports
'til I can see the sun rising in each of them;
then leans over
a long thin strip
of well-worn chamois
dancing ever so lightly
'til the shoes start to burn off
the best shine ever
for the least bit of brown
for two swaying feet
from the other side of town.

Prostates Growing

No man-hating avenger
could situate it better,
turgid bulb at the root
and no old guy's friend;
reclining, bearing down
'til the once proud early morning
fount is strangled to a sizzle.

In silence after heavy rain
you can hear prostates growing,
or being staved
with rinses that turn the hair jet-black,
or irrigation lines that nourish
transplanted hair,
trips to the squash court
squeezed around days
designed to be tubular.

Just as we go to the ballgame
to see players looking bigger
and smaller
we hope to make it through
the operation under spinal block,
the last great reaming of the body
a man's mind can
comprehend.

The Consultant

Jovial in a rumpled white coat,
huge bald head beaded with procedural sweat
our gastroenterology staff-man
we nicknamed 'G.I. Joseph'.
After his own bout of cancer, he too wore a 'bag',
as we were reminded whenever his intestines gurgled
in fearsome borborygmi.

He showed us all his tricks with the long vinyl tube
that encased the fiberoptic miracle.
those were "seat-of-your-pants" days
before autoclaves and AIDS—
He was professionally chipper
talking a nervous young man
through swallowing that garden hose.
Once in, he had us relish the little resistant "pop"
when the sphincter around the stomach gave way,
our patient going, going gone —
valium in his veins and gag reflex stilled
by a spray or two of local
as we eased down into his innards.
"This video camera
designed by an elephant,
like that slowly sinking elevator
in 'She's So Heavy' from *Abbey Road*."
Unmarried, childless,
ever the consultant, Dr. G.I. Joseph
sensed his fleeting importance in a patient's life.
"I'm just a gurgle
in the mainstream of medicine."

Spectator Sports

Can boxing or pro ball rival a tennis match
of over-forty-fivers? Stiff backs and taut hamstrings,
braced knees and groins are on the line,
with not so much as a stress-test
to grant the muster
of competing?

Baseball caps and Tilley hats hug slick domes
nodding onto the blazing court.

They could be wading in a placid lake
eyeing shadowy rock bass
fishing poles at the ready,
or cracking jokes and sunflower seeds
on a beach strewn with inflatables.
Reading by the remains of a fire
in a screened cabin with a three-cup teapot
could be respite from the deadlines
awaiting them in town.

Don't they know better, these Sunday athletes,
girded in gym shorts and a second skin of sun-block,
charging the net in mid-August
on a court of boldly drawn white lines
in the glare of high noon?

The Review that Kills

The review that kills finds the poet at home
alone on a wintry night, furnace on the blink,
three months into a trial separation,
his best friend—so he thought—departed,
two thirds into the second six-pack,
sifting through better reviews from the past.

Who is this 'crickit' who pens the review that kills?
A fellow amateur failed in love or art?
A woman with impossible standards, an ex-lover with a grudge,
Another expert trying to stake out a claim?
Is it the man who, asked if his journal would consider light verse,
answered "Not as long as I am editor."

After the burial, friends and acquaintances denounce
the review that killed; how a sensitive man
with whom they had shared the six-packs of respite
succumbed to a masterful blow
at his history and quirky humor,
the un-ethnic way he spelled his first name,
how he refused to write mainly for his own tribe
and be one more minor poet
from some mountainous village overseas.

Friends gather for a few drinks and a memorial reading,
of the very work that was savaged,
silently comparing their own poems
to those of the unsung martyr, dead
by his own tippy hand, by something
approaching choice;
while somewhere, in the lull
of one more passing season,
the same devout reviewer reloads —

The Russian System
for J.

"*Sistema*".
An unpretty mongrel
it was born of two attempts on Stalin's life.
Uncle Joe sent special bodyguards across the world
to raid the best of every martial art,
and, though later he killed his top men,
what they learned got passed to undercover forces,
the *Spetznaz*.

Now, émigré instructor Mr.Vitaliy
asks his class, "Vwhich do you vwant to learn today,
knives or gons?
Or mebbe khow to take down moltiple attackirs
in beeg crowd, so even TV kameras cannot pik up
Vwhat is khappening."

I can see it now, as a stocky figure
twists and turns through the crowd, shouting the equivalent of
"Excuse me, pardon me, just passing through!"
in his wake shoulders separating shoulders,
knees undoing knees,
people mysteriously dropping like flies,
a mini-massacre.

"Next vik ve stody attack from back seat of taxi,
end attack by pack of dogs."
Yielding to whatever may come,
with a swift response twice as hard
from the other side.

It can drive a black belt crazy.
"It's like fighting with a joker.
They don't face you straight on,
just offer themselves sideways,
or they lounge about, looking
easy-going, hands at their hips.

When they slap, they look like girls fighting
except when you get slapped on the side of the head,
you *stay* slapped;
effective as a late-night phone book on the head
of a Czech, Hungarian or Pole.
Always they go for pressure-points
And kill-zones.

They take you down by your *fingers*,
For Chrissake,
It doesn't look like a martial art.
Though it looks like nothing else."

Mr. Vitaliy has his students wear army fatigues.
"Rossia hez long long border wit manyi manyi enyemies,
manyi deeffirent pipples, kwho fight manyi deeffirent vays.
Dat iz vwhy Da Rossian System most be vithout form,
end izzy to teach."

The attrition rate is high.
It's hard for beginners to
'spar' in such gracelessly mortal art.
Less defensive than hunkering down in deep snow
for one more Nazi convoy to break,
less forward than a race
to send up a dog in a sputnik.

In today's Russia most fights are over greenbacks.
Korruptsiya calls often on tourists to donate a *vzyatka.*
Bags are held up in airports as over-limit,
forty dollars U.S. the improvised fine,
the same bags that easily passed the test
on the way into the country,
though swollen with bottles of imported water,
emptied long before this new weigh-in
on the way out.

We make Mr. Vitaliy proud
and invert the attacker's momentum.
"This Russian couple here didn't have to pay a cent!
Weigh our bags next to theirs!"
Our lips curl, but not in smiles,
as we feel survival
exact its toll.

Climbing Pedro

Soapsuds

Young Samuel scoops
palmfuls of soapsuds
then wipes them off on me,
laughing his head off
at my contaminated state.
Yuck! I cry, playing along
(he's suspiciously neat at meal-time,
and never messes with
his potty)

But what if something happened
while he was fast asleep;
if I were fried in the fuselage of a small plane
or disappeared into a great foreign war?
Years later he'd tell his therapist,
"Of course, I have no memory
of the man,
never really knew him;
I was so young . . ."

Yet here we are: him tossing water into the air
'til he's lifted out kicking,
wanting the bath
to go on forever—
As he hides behind his yellow towel
the two of us carry on
like we'll always be a team,
not noticing those thousands
of gleaming soapsuds,
snapping.

Question of Vitamins

Lunch at The Mars,
squall jacket over my green surgical top.

One table over, this guy in a golf jacket
with a second man old enough to be his father,
a man with nothing in his gray eyes,
and shoulders so round
they look stuffed,
or on leave from a hospital.
The young one tries to cheer him up.
"Dem docs, they don' like you takin' vitamins.
All they do is put you on these dangerous
drugs . . ."
And when he keeps on staring —

"True, it's not for everyone.
But, say a guy needs more B-7, or say B-6,
then that's just what he *needs*."
And when there's still no response,
he kneads the old man's arm.

"For some reason *your* brain needs more
of these vitamins.
I mean, they tell you,
'you don't *need* vitamins, your body makes its *own*."

"Who are they kiddin'?
It's like sayin', 'Don't bother puttin' oil in your car,
just wait till you run out.'
Like, Sandy knows this lady
who gave birth to a baby
who was short of B-vitamins. *Short.*
So how can they say you don't need extra,
that maybe *your patickular body*
don't need extra? So I axe 'em,
does a body need vitamins,
or *don't* it?

He pushes on, a mix of hope and hate.

"Someday, what you're gonna see is *this*:
They're gonna charge people who smoke
and who *don't* take vitamins *more*
for their life insurance,
and people who don't smoke
and who *do* take vitamins, *less.*"
I'm about to start in on my microwaved blintzes
when, sudden as a creak in a hinge,
the huge mountain of a father,
whose featureless back is all that stands
between me and mr. Vitamins, says,

"Whadda you know?
You got a job?"

Miss Karyn McNally's Face

Miss Karyn McNally's dark-maned face
appears overnight along Spadina,
painted against a straw-textured background,
on leaflets taped to green steel pillar after pillar
by her portraitist, selling lessons in classical art.
It has been raining for three days
and on each leaflet, cold sweat not her own
streaks down her graceful neck
to soak her loose-fitting camel cashmere.
The elements wrinkle her fine features.
They paste MILK posters over her
yet she pushes through,
and each weekend her dogged artist
returns to post a fresh round of Karyns.

To the south, in an odd month for publicity,
William Jefferson Clinton marked the White House
with rancid sperm that sent republican wolves
into a frenzy.
Something about the face of the fallen Adonis
from a place called Hope
displayed in a million aspects of contrition
kept raising his standing in the polls.
I think of this on my way to work,
and of Monica's ubiquitous face.

How many will take down
Miss McNally's portraits plastered
across the city's lampposts as though she were Wanted
for their own private viewing:
marginal men, starved for a woman's touch,
businessmen too harrowed to recall
the image of a young wife,
all walking past a female gaze
that radiates the vulnerable dignity
of one forced to hold a pose.
How sorely wanted is your beauty
on this damp loveless winter day.

My Dentist Hands Me a Mirror

My dentist hands me a mirror
to show how a little ridge of gum
projects over a frontal crown,
in a protest of violet.
But something in the fluorescent light,
head tilted back,
mouth gaping in a wide O,
reflects the face of a corpse.

I would call it a death mask
but it is more a flask
drained by too urgent swallowing
to the tuneless suck of a vacuum hose
and the shriek of a high-tech de-scaler.
(Is this why my friends fear dentists?)

The face is that of a crock, a gomer,
a no-hoper, body-bagger,
piss-poor-protoplasm-poorly-put-together,
the intern's pet-names
for the dead and the dying.

Yet soon the blood-flecked bib comes off,
and, balding man with the close-cropped beard,
I arise from the hired throne
to rejoin the living,
on wizened lips, a cleaner
more effortful smile.

Order in the Condo
for R.

Order has been restored.
Since the day he inexplicably turned orange,
Pedro, my son's three foot iguana
with sharp teeth and lashing tail
no longer patrols the guestroom we surrendered.
Now, like a piece of kinetic sculpture
he postures and poses in the new floor-to-ceiling pen
that ate up the dining-room 'el'.
Still, when I approach he charges
with bulging eyes and puffed wattles,
macho immigrant to a cold country
asked to settle for less than his home in the sun.

Similarly displaced, my own
Santa Maria, the Maltese,
kept swallowing $600 fur balls
and setting off my asthma.
Inhalers neutralized her nights on my pillow.
When she deserted, on doctor's orders I chose
Iggy, the hypo-allergenic *bichon frise*,
a lovable matted dust-mop with legs,
but on one walk he broke loose,
another big-city casualty.

These days my son is never home,
styling hair into the wee hours
or off somewhere with his guy friends
or his personal trainer,
running up frightening VISA bills.

Last week, one lonely night,
disheartened after a day of sending off résumés,
I heard the wire cage rustle and looked up:
Pedro's long curved talons pulled him
to human-eye level. He hissed
three words perhaps confessional
but more likely aimed at me.
Just three words, twice
through closed eyes, head nodding mechanically
as if to launch them up my spine:
Childless by choice, he hissed,
Childless by choice.

Still Life

She leans over the mantle gazing
into a sheen of glass reflecting
a poster of a Joseph Cornell exhibit,
an elegant *infanta* princess
captive in an open armoire, her delicate hand
caressing a small red ball.

She is between clients,
gnawing gingerly at a thick-crusted turkey wedge
on an open sheet of waxed paper.
She guards a pegged front tooth; three years ago she sneezed
and watched her pearly-white
fly through the air;
another three hours in the dentist's chair.

Beside her sandwich on the mantle, a *New Yorker*
The Fiction Edition, *the fiction addiction,*
respite from the usual fare.
Between bites she samples an old interview with Beckett,
who claims to know no more about Godot than we do.
Through closed eyes:
How needy/ of Didi/ and Gogo/ to attend Godot.
"Too many syllables, name-dropping, and the rhythm is wrong,"
chides a workshop coach from an earlier time.

In every sense surrounded by this work day,
the book club selection a life away.
Though in the glass of the Cornell she sees reflected
the flying buttresses of a Sixties-modern elementary school
set against a clear blue sky,
a clamour of children being released
into the full noon.
Their voices waft through the one window that still opens.
"Sky-blue, sky-blue, who's It?"

Not you.

The Wound
for Joseph Brodsky

At a graduate student book-sale
I found your weighty collection of essays, *Less Than One.*
On the back cover a leonine photo of you,
you still had hair
and looked just this side of pissed off.
They had stuck a price-tag across your left upper forehead
that read $16.99,
more than I paid for your remarkable company.
I turned the book over and calculated the original mark-up,
(there's always a mark-up from the U.S. to Canada
—let alone darkest Russia,
far in excess of exchange rates).
I started peeling the book-sale price-tag, not knowing
its gummy backing would refuse to lift
but rather, divided like onionskin
leaving a white film,
a shrapnel wound to the head,
or a clump of old matted bandages
at which I scraped with my nails
for the better part of an hour, to free
the Nobel laureate brow,
wondering, Do I dare use water?
Will I want to make a gift of this book
once I'm through, as if one has ever had enough
of a mind like yours.
I will work away, till I reclaim the image
of a better writer, a propriety
for which you would have had little use,
having borne your wounds as a matter of fact.

Evening Prayers in August

Tonight I am a man
vacationing with family,
the caseload a distant memory.
A folding cot claims the floor space
in this dark cramped motel, forces me
to read in the bathroom,
perched on the toilet lid
in a patch of orange light
while my daughter tries
to push off into sleep.
Soon she and my wife
will be snoring in synchrony,
our son one room down the hall
with his *zayde,*
already sleeping so deeply
that tomorrow he'll ambush us
with wakefulness.

Chlorine eats at my eyes.
Whatever my antibiotic can't kill,
this motel pool will.
Unable to turn on more light,
or resort to the ecstasy
of wasting kleenex and water,
my thoughts drift
to evils that can follow us anywhere —
when suddenly a finger of white light
slices my visual field!
I jerk up at the pale garotte
across the shower:
a bone-dry swimsuit
is still laking in one corner,
on the verge of a second
animation!

Storm at Huntington Lakes

From the porch of a seniors condo
we watch the looming stormfront hit,
sheeting the landscape with wave on wave of rain
that shivers and shakes the great wall of hedge
sculpted from the waists of ficus trees
throwing about their thick arms like pentecostals
as cocoanut palms and palmettos speed the pace
of the frantic revival with stretched green spheres
and floppy fans bulging like inverted umbrellas.
Even the Australian pines start teetering,
their tall trunks forget gently swaying ways,
wishing they were sturdy royal palms
or cocoanut trees meant to bend with the elements,
to make it through to the afterstorm,
the promised land of mature identities,
though with one eye always open
for exactly where those fine fruits fell.

Bringing Home Buttons

I knew I would have to learn Doglish,
But to rethink a world view . . .

Pride of my daughter's five-year campaign,
you look like a little raccoon in your frizzled black coat
with white mukluks on three paws,
tricolour sheltie with tan eyebrows,
you romp and leap and herd us.

Within minutes of your arrival
you grind the shoelace tip from my pricey Clarke cariboo
and after crunching your kibble, leave behind
supernovae on the hardwood floor
and squeeze down-to-earth asteroids
while we frantically thumb the *Complete Idiot's Guide.*

Our once hermetically sealed house
you lace with puppy pee/wet fur
smelling somewhere between talcum powder
and the dented wet rubber ball you paw
as you slip and yelp down kitchen alley.
Soon your long black and white hairs will be everywhere.
Nor will I walk another day
without plastic rustling in my pants pocket.

Cute as a Button, or Buttons 'n Bows,
or whatever the Registry okays for a name,
what do you care that few good poems are written
about bringing home a puppy,
no matter how that act against metaphor
protects a poet's sanity?

To see the world, for a time, as obliging,
and real, real as
a little black tail with white tip
brushing across a bare foot —
Though after gazing down, my neck snaps upwards,
contentment being a form of writer's block.

Epilogue: Open Casket

Open Casket

She presides over the red-carpeted parlour,
patrolled by her five devoted sisters
who pass around photos from better days.

The bearded doctor, a guest of her middle sister Michelle,
looks pale, his own tradition frowning
on preserving the husk, on efforts to transform
our stony paste into a figure from a wax museum.

"Would you like to come see Nadine?"

He demurs, but steps forward, having never met in real life
this remarkable lawyer.
Cancer took four years to vanquish
her cantankerous drive to remain,
her bones crumbling, iron rods reinforcing hips, and neck.

The pretty spectre in lipstick and cropped hair,
flat-chested without prostheses,
seems asleep in an eternal dress-suit
beneath white lilies.
He imagines lifting her frail hand,
her fingers gloved by a second skin.

"Nadine was something of an athlete,"
whispers the oldest sister, Marianne.
"She insisted we blend for her those carrot drinks
till the end, and we were happy to.
Once she learned how to walk again
we couldn't keep her away from her gardening.
She may have needed a walker,
but she surfed the Net and planned the family vacations.
Finally she left us, after a fall
from her bed during a dream.

As they turn, Michelle takes the doctor's arm.
"I'm not sure," he says, "about such open display"
"We can see her, touch her. Kiss.
We can feel her gone"
A child hesitates, touches her mother's shoulder
with reverence, then dashes off
to keep up with her cousins.